Reading Quick Checks

Table of Contents

Introduction

Program Overview

The *Benchmark Advance* program has ten units per grade in Grades K–6. Each three-week unit focuses on a Unit Concept, such as "Technology and Society" or "Point of View," a grade-appropriate topic, and an Essential Question. Each unit provides reading selections related to the topic and Essential Question. Instruction in each unit focuses on reading comprehension and building language, word study, and writing.

The *Reading Quick Checks* assessments are based on the reading skills taught in the *Benchmark Advance* program. There are two assessments for each skill. Skills in this book follow the same sequence as the *Benchmark Advance Intervention Reading* lessons in each grade and are organized in two sections: "Literature" and "Informational Text." The Resource Map on pages iv–v aligns the skills being assessed to the *Benchmark Advance Intervention Reading* lessons.

Administering the Quick Check Assessments

Each assessment focuses on a single skill and is intended for individual administration, although these assessments may also be used with small or large groups. We recommend that you make a copy of the Quick Check for each student you plan to assess. Have the student write his or her name and the date at the top of the page. If needed, read or review the directions at the top of the page with the student. Then have the student complete the activity by writing or marking answers on the page itself, on the back of the page, or on a separate sheet of paper. The way students respond to questions varies, based on the types of questions and the page format.

Every assessment may be used more than once, if needed. If a student does not do well on an assessment the first time, you may want to assess the student again with the same activity. Or you may use the two assessments per skill in different combinations. For example, you may administer the two skill Quick Checks as a pretest and posttest, at the beginning and end of the quarter; or as an initial test and follow-up retest to see how much progress the student has made.

The two assessments for each skill use different reading passages and may use different item formats to assess the same skill. This approach provides variety and more reliable assessment. In most cases, Quick Check B may be slightly more difficult than Quick Check A. Some reading passages appear more than once. Each time a reading passage appears, it is used to assess a different reading skill.

Quick Check to Reading Intervention

To score each Quick Check, refer to the Answer Keys in the back of the book. Every question is worth 1 point unless otherwise indicated in the answer key. In questions with more than one expected response, each correct answer is worth 1 point. (For example, a question that asks students to underline two detail sentences in the passage is worth 2 points.) Each assessment has a score box on the page; it indicates the total number of points possible for the particular Quick Check. You may use the score box to record the results of the assessment.

The score on each Quick Check may be used for record keeping or grading, but the final score on each page is less important than how the student responds along the way. Ultimately, these Quick Checks are formative assessments to help you monitor students' progress and adapt instruction to individual needs. When assessments indicate that intervention is called for, use the Resource Map on pages iv–v to identify the appropriate *Benchmark Advance Intervention Reading* lesson.

If the student scores...	Then...
between 80% and 100%	Move on to the next Quick Check or skill.
between 66% and 80%	Consider administering the Quick Check again. Continue monitoring the student during future Quick Checks.
below 66%	Use additional resources shown in the Resource Map to provide the student with opportunities to remediate skills.

Grade 2
Reading Quick Checks Resource Map

Name _____ Date _____

Directions: Read the passage and answer the questions.
Write your answers on separate paper or on the back of this page.

Rabbit's Day

1   Rabbit liked to find out things. She hopped through the field and the <u>woods</u> looking here and there. Sometimes she got into trouble.

2   One day, she saw a bee fly into a log. "What is that bee doing?" she asked herself. When she poked her nose into the log, angry bees came out. They buzzed, "Keep out of here! This is our home!"

3   Next, Rabbit saw a cave and looked inside. She saw something very big and black. "Go back where you came from!" said the bear. "This is my home!"

4   Then Rabbit spotted a hole in the ground. She poked her head inside. A snake hissed, "Get away!"

5   Rabbit felt a little sad because no one wanted her company. Then she smelled something sweet. She followed the smell back to her own home. Her mom said, "Have some nice fresh lettuce with me."

✓ **Comprehension Questions**

1. **Where does this story take place?**
   Underline the sentence that tells.

2. **What does Rabbit find in the log?**

3. **Who does Rabbit meet next?**

4. **Circle the sentence that tells why Rabbit feels sad.**   ____/4

Name _____ Date _____

Directions: Read the passage and answer the questions.
Write your answers on separate paper or on the back of this page.

Taki's Present

1   "Where is my piggy bank?" Taki asked. Tomorrow was Mom's birthday, and he wanted to buy her a birthday present.

2   His room was piled with clothes and toys, so he put everything away. But he did not find his bank.

3   Next, he went to his brother's room. It was a mess, too. He straightened everything up but found no piggy bank.

4   Then he looked for his dad in the kitchen. Dad wasn't there, but the kitchen was a mess. Taki began washing the dirty dishes.

5   Just then, his mom walked into the kitchen. "Taki, what have you done?" She peered into the boys' rooms and then gave Taki a big hug. "This is the BEST birthday present ever!"

✓ **Comprehension Questions**

1. **Where does this story take place?**

2. **What did Taki do in his room?**
   Underline the sentence that tells.

3. **What did Taki do next?**

4. **Circle the sentence that tells why Taki goes into the kitchen.**

____/4

Name _____ Date _____

Directions: Read the passage and answer the questions.
Write your answers on separate paper or on the back of this page.

Turtle and Frog

1 Turtle lived in a pond with Frog. Turtle wanted to be friends, but Frog was not interested.

2 One day, Frog was showing off. He swam through the water like a water bug. Everyone said, "Ooohh!"

3 Frog said, "Turtle, if you can swim like that, I might like you."

4 Turtle was a good swimmer, so he swam quickly through the water like a fish. Everyone said, "Wow!"

5 Frog didn't like that. So he flipped on his back and swam around. Then he dared Turtle to do the same.

6 When Turtle flipped over, he could not move. Frog started laughing. He splashed water on Turtle, who began to sink. "Okay, Frog, you win," said Turtle.

7 "I'm still not your friend," Frog said.

8 "That's okay," Turtle said. "Who would want a friend like you?"

 Comprehension Questions

1. Circle the sentence that tells where the story takes place.

2. What does Turtle want at the beginning of the story?
    Underline the sentence that tells.

3. Why does Frog laugh at Turtle?

4. What does Turtle decide at the end?

_____/4

Name _____ Date _____

Directions: Read the passage and answer the questions.
Write your answers on separate paper or on the back of this page.

Mouse's Tail

1   Mouse had a very short tail. One night as he went to bed, he wished his tail would grow. Then he fell asleep.

2   In a dream, Mouse saw his friends. He asked them to pull his tail to make it longer. They pulled and pulled, and soon it was twice as long!

3   Someone said, "Now your legs are too short!" So they pulled his legs until they were very long.

4   Someone else said, "Now your ears are too little." His friends pulled his ears until they were very large.

5   Mouse looked at himself. He said, "But now I don't look like a mouse!"

6   Suddenly, Mouse's mother was shaking him. "Wake up," she said. "You are dreaming!" Mouse woke up. His tail was still short, but his legs and ears were just right. He looked just like a mouse!

✓ **Comprehension Questions**

1.   **Where does this story take place?**

2.   **What does Mouse wish for? Underline the sentence that tells.**

3.   **What happens after Mouse goes to bed?**

4.   **Who wakes Mouse up? Circle the sentence that tells.**

____/4

Name _____ Date _____

Directions: Read the passage and answer the questions.
Write your answers on separate paper or on the back of this page.

Ravi's Bear

1   Ravi's mom bought her a stuffed bear at the store. Then Ravi took a bus home, but she left the bear on the bus. When she returned home, the toy was missing!

2   The bus driver saw the bear. He stuffed it into his backpack, but it fell out onto the sidewalk.

3   A boy on a bicycle saw the bear and stopped. He put the bear in his basket and rode to the park. While he was playing, a dog pulled the bear out of the basket and ran.

4   A man was delivering groceries. He stopped the dog and took the bear from it. Holding the bear under his arm, he delivered groceries to a house.

5   Ravi answered the door. "Mama!" she cried. "The grocery man is here, and he has my bear!" The man smiled happily and handed the bear to Ravi.

✓ **Comprehension Questions**

1. **What happens first in the story?**
2. **How does the boy on the bicycle get the bear?**
3. **How does the man with groceries get the bear?**
4. **Tell how Ravi gets her bear back in the end.**

____/4

Name _____ Date _____

Directions: Read the passage and answer the question.
Write your answers on separate paper or on the back of this page.

Sammy's Acorns

1   Sammy Squirrel was dashing back and forth gathering acorns. Sally Squirrel wondered what he was doing, so she stopped him. "Why are you rushing about?" she asked.

2   "I'm putting acorns away for the winter," Sammy said. "It will be cold soon, and the snow will fall."

3   Sally said, "Let me help. How many do you need?"

4   "I think I need one hundred acorns to get me through the cold days," he said.

5   So Sammy and Sally worked together. Soon they had one hundred acorns in Sammy's cozy nest.

6   "What about you?" Sammy asked. "Where are you keeping your acorns?"

7   Sally scratched her head. She said, "I forgot about the winter! I don't have one acorn."

8   Sammy said, "Let's get going then. We can gather your acorns in no time!"

 Comprehension Question

Tell what happens in this story in your own words. Be sure to include more than three events from the story.   ____/4

Name _____ Date _____

Directions: Read the passage and answer the questions.
Write your answers on separate paper or on the back of this page.

The Crow and the Pigeons

1   One day Crow saw a flock of pigeons in the town square. People were feeding them peanuts. Crow wanted some peanuts. But people did not like crows and would not feed him.

2   So Crow painted his black feathers gray and white like the pigeons. Then he flew down and enjoyed the feast. People fed him more and more peanuts. He was so happy that he called out, "Caw! Caw!"

3   Then the pigeons knew Crow didn't belong with them. In anger, the pigeons pecked at him. So Crow had to fly away. He spotted his flock in a tree and flew over to it.

4   When the other crows saw the gray and white bird, they made loud noises. They said, "We don't know who you are! Go away!" Then the flock flew away and left him alone.

5   Crow decided, "It's best just to be yourself."

 Comprehension Questions

1. **Why does Crow pretend to be a pigeon? Underline the sentence that tells.**

2. **How do the pigeons act toward Crow?**

3. **How do the other crows treat Crow?**

4. **Underline the sentence that tells the message or moral of the story.**

____/4

Name _____ Date _____

Directions: Read the passage and answer the questions.
Write your answers on separate paper or on the back of this page.

The Donkey and A Load of Salt

1   A man loaded some large bags of salt on the back of his donkey. Then they walked toward town. When they crossed a stream, the donkey tripped and fell into the water. The salt melted, and the donkey's load got much lighter.

2   The next day, the man loaded the donkey up with salt again. But when they reached the stream, the donkey lay in the water. Again, most of the salt melted. His load got much lighter.

3   On the third day, the man loaded the salt on the donkey. But he also added a bag of sponges. At the stream, the donkey lay in the water again. Then he rolled over so the salt would melt. But this time, the sponges filled with water. When the donkey tried to walk, his load was heavier than ever.

4   Donkey thought, "You can fool a wise man once, but a second time will surely fail."

✓ **Comprehension Questions**

1.   What did the donkey learn when he fell into the water the first time? Underline the sentence that tells.

2.   What did the donkey do the next day?

3.   What happened to the donkey on the third day?

4.   What is the lesson or moral that the donkey learns?   ___/4

Name _____ Date _____

Directions: Read the passage and answer the questions.
Write your answers on separate paper or on the back of this page.

The Day Snake Flew

1   Snake could climb trees and swim in the river. But he was not happy because he wanted to fly.

2   One day, Snake saw Eagle flying high in the air. He should have hidden, but he could not take his eyes off the bird. Eagle spotted Snake and grabbed him in her claws. Then she soared up into the air.

3   "Good thing I saw you!" Eagle said. "I'm hungry!"

4   Snake was scared and tried to get free. He swung his body this way and that. He screamed for help.

5   Eagle flew toward her nest. When she got near, her babies became afraid. Snake was thrashing back and forth and yelling. One eaglet tried to fly out of the nest. Of course, she was too young to fly.

6   So Eagle had to drop Snake to rescue her baby. She caught her eaglet and returned to the nest.

7   Snake landed on the ground and was very glad to be there. He never wanted to fly after that.

✓ **Comprehension Questions**

1.   **What did Snake do to try to get away from Eagle? Underline the <u>two</u> sentences that tell.**

2.   **What did the baby eagle do when she saw Snake?**

3.   **How did Eagle save her baby?**

4.   **How did Snake feel when he landed on the ground?**

_____/5

Name _____ Date _____

Directions: Read the passage and answer the questions.
Write your answers on separate paper or on the back of this page.

Dan's Bike

1   Dan owned an old bike. It often broke. One day, his chain broke. So he took it to Ana's Bike Shop.

2   "Can you fix it, Ana?" he asked.

3   "I don't have time," Ana said. "But you can fix it yourself." Ana showed Dan what to do, and he fixed the chain.

4   Then his front tire went flat. He went back to Ana's shop. "Sorry," she said. "I'm very busy." But Ana showed him what to do, and Dan fixed the flat tire.

5   Next, his brakes stopped working. He rolled his bike into Ana's shop.

6   Ana said, "I'm really busy, but I can give you a tool to tighten the brakes. You can do it yourself." So Dan fixed the brakes by himself.

7   When he finished, Ana said, "Do you want a job? You know a lot about bikes, and I need a helper!"

✓ **Comprehension Questions**

1. **Where did Dan go when his chain broke? Underline the sentence that tells.**
2. **What did Dan do when he got a flat tire?**
3. **Why did Dan go back to Ana's shop a third time?**
4. **What did Ana do after Dan fixed his own brakes?**

____/4

Name _____ Date _____

Directions: Read the poem and answer the question.
Write your answers on separate paper or on the back of this page.

A Close Call

Waiting and watching

From the top of a tree,

A hawk spies a bunny—

No, two, no, now three!

5   The hawk dives for dinner,

Delightful and near,

But the bunnies see the bird

And are filled with fear.

Hippity, hippity,

10   Hippity, hop,

They run for the woods

And dare not stop.

 Comprehension Question

**In each of the three verses, underline the words that use
alliteration (words that have the same beginning sound).**

_____/3

          Grade 2 • Benchmark Advance • Reading Quick Checks • © Benchmark Education Company, LLC

Name _____ Date _____

Directions: Read the poem and answer the question.
Write your answers on separate paper or on the back of this page.

Polly Pig

Polly Pig was hungry

and she knew what to do,

She left her little pig pen

to have lunch with Farmer Sue.

5   Farmer Sue said, "Hey, Polly,

I've got food for you."

She served beans and beets,

With some mushy peas, too.

"Yippee," yelled Polly,

10   "I just love these peas,

But next time please add

Some nice chunks of cheese."

 Comprehension Question

**In each of the three verses, underline the words that use
alliteration (words that have the same beginning sound).**

_____/3

Name _____ Date _____

Directions: Read the poems and answer the questions.
Write your answers on separate paper or on the back of this page.

The Mouse and the Lion

A poor thing the mouse was, and yet,

When the Lion got caught in a net,

All his strength was no use,

'Twas the little poor mouse

5   Who chewed his way out of the net.

The Tortoise and the Hare

'Twas a race between Tortoise and Hare

Hare thought she had much time to spare,

So she lay down to sleep,

And let old Tortoise creep

5   To the finish line first, by a hair.

 Comprehension Questions

1.   In "The Mouse and the Lion," put a check mark above each
       word or syllable you should stress as you read.

2.   How is the rhythm in both of these poems alike?

3.   Which lines rhyme in each of the poems?   ____/3

Name _____ Date _____

Directions: Read the poem and answer the questions.
Write your answers on separate paper or on the back of this page.

Afternoon On A Hill

by Edna St. Vincent Millay

I will be the gladdest thing

    Under the sun!

I will touch a hundred flowers

    And not pick one.

5   I will look at cliffs and clouds

    With quiet eyes,

Watch the wind bow down the grass,

    And the grass rise.

And when lights begin to show

10   Up from the town,

I will mark which must be mine,

    And then start down!

 Comprehension Questions

1. **In the first verse, put a check mark above each word or syllable you should stress as you read.**

2. **How is the rhythm in first and third lines in each verse different from the rhythm in the second and fourth lines?**

3. **Which lines rhyme in this poem?**   ____/3

Name _____ Date _____

Directions: Read the passage and answer the questions.
Write your answers on separate paper or on the back of this page.

I Write About The Butterfly

by Louisa May Alcott

I write about the butterfly,

It is a pretty thing;

And flies about like the birds,

But it does not sing.

5   First it is a little grub,

And then it is a nice yellow cocoon,

And then the butterfly

Eats its way out soon.

They live on dew and honey,

10   They do not have any hive,

They do not sting like wasps, and bees, and hornets,

And to be as good as they are we should strive.

 Comprehension Questions

1. **How is the butterfly different from a bird?**

2. **What are the steps in a butterfly's growth? Underline the lines of the poem that explain.**

3. **How are butterflies different from wasps and bees?**

4. **What does the last line of the poem suggest?**

____/4

Name _____ Date _____

Directions: Read the poem and answer the questions.
Write your answers on separate paper or on the back of this page.

Travel

by Edna St. Vincent Millay

The railroad track is miles away,

And the day is loud with voices speaking,

Yet there isn't a train goes by all day

But I hear its whistle shrieking.

5   All night there isn't a train goes by,

Though the night is still for sleep and dreaming

But I see its cinders red on the sky,

And hear its engine steaming.

My heart is warm with the friends I make,

10   And better friends I'll not be knowing,

Yet there isn't a train I wouldn't take,

No matter where it's going.

Comprehension Questions

1.   **Underline two lines of the poem that use repetition.**

2.   **Circle the line in the second verse that uses alliteration.**

3.   **How does the speaker in the poem feel about her friends?**

4.   **How does the speaker feel about trains? Tell how you know.**   ____/4

Name _____ Date _____

Directions: Read the passage and answer the questions.
Write your answers on separate paper or on the back of this page.

Getting Better

1   Tanya wanted to play soccer with her brother Ray and his friends.

2   "You don't know how to play soccer," said Ray.

3   Tanya took her soccer ball and played by herself.

4   Every day Tanya asked Ray to let her play. Every day he said, "You don't know how to play."

5   Tanya's mother saw her in the backyard and showed her how to kick the ball better. She taught her how to steal the ball and how to pass. Tanya kept playing every day.

6   One day Mom said to Ray, "Let her play. She might surprise you."

7   Tanya darted this way and that. She made passes, stole the ball, and almost scored.

8   Ray's friend said to him, "Your sister is good! Did you teach her how to play?"

✓ **Comprehension Questions**

1.   **What does Tanya want at the beginning of the story? Underline the sentence that tells.**

2.   **What is the problem at the beginning of the story?**

3.   **What does Tanya do in the beginning of the story?**

_____/3

Name _____ Date _____

Directions: Read the passage and answer the questions.
Write your answers on separate paper or on the back of this page.

The Missing Tail

1   Dragon was friends with Squirrel, Snake, and Robin.
Dragon was big, and she could fly. But her friends
liked to tease her. One day they hid behind a
rock. When she walked by, they jumped out and
surprised her. She flew up into a tree with fright.

2   A crow saw her in the tree and said, "What
happened to your tail, Dragon?"

3   Dragon looked back and didn't see her tail.
She said, "I must have dropped it."

4   "I've got it!" Squirrel squeaked.

5   "No, I have it!" Robin peeped.

6   "I have it!" Snake hissed. "I'm not giving it back!"

7   Dragon got so mad that she stretched her wings
and flew down to the ground. On the way, she
saw her tail plain as day. It had been hiding
between her legs all that time!

8   Dragon laughed. "What silly friends I have!"

✓ **Comprehension Questions**

1.   Underline the sentence that tells what Dragon's friends do to tease her.

2.   What is Dragon's problem in the first paragraph of the story?

3.   What does Dragon do in the beginning of the story?

 ____/3

Name _____ Date _____

Directions: Read the passage and answer the questions.
Write your answers on separate paper or on the back of this page.

The Bike

1   Misha wanted to ride her new bike, but she was afraid. So she asked her father to hold the back of the bike as she rode.

2   "Are you holding me?" she asked.

3   "I'm holding you!" he answered. Misha began to pedal. She wobbled but rode ten feet down the path. Then she put on the brakes.

4   "Let's try again!" Misha said. "Are you holding on?"

5   "I am," her father said. His hand lightly rested on the seat. Misha rode all the way down the path.

6   "One more time!" Misha yelled. "Don't forget to hold me!"

7   But Misha's father knew better. He ran behind her but let go after a few feet. Misha sailed down the path with a big smile on her face.

8   "The next time you can let go!" Misha said.

9   Her father smiled. "I already did!"

✓ **Comprehension Questions**

1.   **What is the problem in this story? Underline the sentence that tells.**

2.   **How does Misha's father help her?**

3.   **What happens at the end of the story?**   ____/3

Name _____ Date _____

Directions: Read the passage and answer the questions.
Write your answers on separate paper or on the back of this page.

Tenal's Treasure

1   Tenal and his wife lived in the country. One night, they heard footsteps outside the window. Three men were planning to rob the house!

2   Tenal shouted, "I heard there are robbers nearby."

3   His wife shouted back, "We must hide our gold. Let's put it in the well. No one will find it there."

4   Tenal and his wife carried many loads and dropped them into the well. Later, the robbers went to the well. They hauled up buckets of water and poured it in the garden. Finally, the well was empty. They looked down, but all they saw were stones!

5   Then the robbers saw Tenal and his wife standing nearby. The men were afraid. One said, "Don't put us in jail! We are sorry."

6   Tenal said, "You have helped me by watering my garden. I will let you go if you never steal again."

7   And the robbers never robbed anyone again.

✓ **Comprehension Questions**

1.   **What is the problem in this story? Underline the sentence that tells.**

2.   **How do Tenal and his wife trick the robbers?**

3.   **What happens at the end of the story?**

____/3

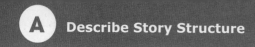
Name _____ Date _____

Directions: Read the passage and answer the questions.
Write your answers on separate paper or on the back of this page.

The Warm Flea

1   The night was cold, and a flea began to shiver. So it jumped on a deer to get warm. But the deer began to scratch. She said, "Get off me. You're making me itch."

2   The flea said, "I'm cold, and your fur is warm."

3   So the deer said, "Hop on that cow. She goes into the barn at night. You'll be warm there."

4   The flea jumped on the cow. But soon it began to scratch. The cow said, "Go hop on that dog. He goes into the house at night. It's warm there."

5   The flea hopped onto the dog. But soon the dog began to itch. He said, "Get off me, flea!" The flea explained that she needed to be warm.

6   So the dog said, "Hop on the man over there. He gets into bed at night, and it is really warm there."

7   The flea jumped onto the man's head. But the man caught the flea and put it outside. And that was that!

✓ **Comprehension Questions**

1.   What does the flea do in the beginning? Circle the sentence that tells.

2.   What **two** things happen in the middle of the story?

3.   How does the story end?

_____/4

Name _____ Date _____

Directions: Read the passage and answer the questions.
Write your answers on separate paper or on the back of this page.

Monkey and the Plums

1 Monkey was very hungry, but he couldn't find any food. He walked and walked, but all the fruit on the trees had already been eaten. Then he reached the river. He looked across it and spotted a plum tree filled with plums.

2 He needed to cross the river, so he stepped on a log. But it was not a log! It was a huge crocodile.

3 Monkey said, "Don't eat me! The King asked me to count all the crocodiles in the river."

4 Crocodile smiled, "The king should know that there are many of us. Wait, and I'll go get everyone."

5 So Crocodile called all the crocodiles, and they filled the river from one side to the other.

6 "Now, I must count you!" Monkey said. So Monkey stepped on crocodile after crocodile until he reached the other side of the river. Then he climbed the plum tree and ate his fill of plums.

Comprehension Questions

1. What is Monkey's first problem in the story? Underline the sentence that tells.

2. What problem does Monkey have next?

3. What <u>two</u> things happen in the middle of the story?

4. How does the story end?

_____/5

Name _____ Date _____

Directions: Read the passage and answer the questions.
Write your answers on separate paper or on the back of this page.

Rabbit's Day

1   Rabbit liked to find out things. She hopped through the field and the woods looking here and there. Sometimes she got into trouble.

2   One day, she saw a bee fly into a log. "What is that bee doing?" she asked herself. When she poked her nose into the log, angry bees came out. They buzzed, "Keep out of here! This is our home!"

3   Next, Rabbit saw a cave and looked inside. She saw something very big and black. "Go back where you came from!" said the bear. "This is my home!"

4   Then Rabbit spotted a hole in the ground. She poked her head inside. A snake hissed, "Get away!"

5   Rabbit felt a little sad because no one wanted her company. Then she smelled something sweet. She followed the smell back to her own home. Her mom said, "Have some nice fresh lettuce with me."

✓ **Comprehension Questions**

1.   How does Rabbit feel when she sees the bee go into a log?

2.   How do the bees feel when Rabbit pokes her nose inside the log?

3.   How does the bear feel when Rabbit peeks in?

4.   Which character is glad to see Rabbit?

____/4

Name _____ Date _____

Directions: Read the passage and answer the questions.
Write your answers on separate paper or on the back of this page.

Turtle and Frog

1   Turtle lived in a pond with Frog. Turtle wanted to be friends, but Frog was not interested.

2   One day, Frog was showing off. He swam through the water like a water bug. Everyone said, "Ooohh!"

3   Frog said, "Turtle, if you can swim like that, I might like you."

4   Turtle was a good swimmer, so he swam quickly through the water like a fish. Everyone said, "Wow!"

5   Frog didn't like that. So he flipped on his back and swam around. Then he dared Turtle to do the same.

6   When Turtle flipped over, he could not move. Frog started laughing. He splashed water on Turtle, who began to sink. "Okay, Frog, you win," said Turtle.

7   "I'm still not your friend," Frog said.

8   "That's okay," Turtle said. "Who would want a friend like you?"

✓ **Comprehension Questions**

1.   **How does Turtle feel about Frog at the beginning of the story?**
2.   **How does Frog feel when Turtle swims like a fish?**
3.   **What does Frog do to trick Turtle?**
4.   **How does Turtle feel about Frog at the end?**

Name _____ Date _____

Directions: Read the passage and answer the questions.
Write your answers on separate paper or on the back of this page.

Taki's Present

1   "Where is my piggy bank?" Taki asked. Tomorrow
was Mom's birthday, and he wanted to buy her a
birthday present.

2   His room was piled with clothes and toys, so he
put everything away. But he did not find his bank.

3   Next, he went to his brother's room. It was a mess,
too. He straightened everything up but found no
piggy bank.

4   Then he looked for his dad in the kitchen. Dad
wasn't there, but the kitchen was a mess. Taki
began washing the dirty dishes.

5   Just then, his mom walked into the kitchen. "Taki,
what have you done?" She peered into the boys'
rooms and then gave Taki a big hug. "This is the
BEST birthday present ever!"

✓ **Comprehension Questions**

1.   **What did Taki want to do at the beginning of the story?
     Underline the sentence that tells.**

2.   **Describe <u>two</u> things Taki does that show he likes things
     to be clean and neat.**

3.   **How did Mom feel about what Taki did?
     Circle the sentence that tells.**   _____/4

Name _____ Date _____

Directions: Read the passage and answer the questions.
Write your answers on separate paper or on the back of this page.

Dan's Bike

1   Dan owned an old bike. It often broke. One day, his chain broke. So he took it to Ana's Bike Shop.

2   "Can you fix it, Ana?" he asked.

3   "I don't have time," Ana said. "But you can fix it yourself." Ana showed Dan what to do, and he fixed the chain.

4   Then his front tire went flat. He went back to Ana's shop. "Sorry," she said. "I'm very busy." But Ana showed him what to do, and Dan fixed the flat tire.

5   Next, his brakes stopped working. He rolled his bike into Ana's shop.

6   Ana said, "I'm really busy, but I can give you a tool to tighten the brakes. You can do it yourself." So Dan fixed the brakes by himself.

7   When he finished, Ana said, "Do you want a job? You know a lot about bikes, and I need a helper!"

✓ **Comprehension Questions**

1.   **How can you tell that Dan likes to learn?**

2.   **Describe <u>two</u> things Ana does that show she wants to help Dan.**

3.   **How can you tell that Ana likes Dan? Circle the sentence that tells.**

____/4

Name _____ Date _____

Directions: Read the passage and answer the questions.
Write your answers on separate paper or on the back of this page.

The Crow and the Pigeons

1   One day Crow saw a flock of pigeons in the town square. People were feeding them peanuts. Crow wanted some peanuts. But people did not like crows and would not feed him.

2   So Crow painted his black feathers gray and white like the pigeons'. Then he flew down and enjoyed the feast. People fed him lots of peanuts. He was so happy that he called out, "Caw! Caw! Caw!"

3   Then the pigeons knew Crow didn't belong with them. In anger, the pigeons pecked at him. So Crow had to fly away. He spotted his flock in a tree and flew over to it.

4   When the other crows saw the gray and white bird, they made loud noises. They said, "We don't know who you are! Go away!" Then the flock flew away and left him alone.

5   Crow thought, "It's best just to be yourself."

 Comprehension Questions

1.   **Where does this story begin? Underline the sentence that tells.**

2.   **Where does Crow go to eat peanuts?**

3.   **Where does Crow go at the end of the story?**
       Circle the sentence that tells.   ____/3

Name _____ Date _____

Directions: Read the passage and answer the questions.
Write your answers on separate paper or on the back of this page.

Tenal's Treasure

1   Tenal and his wife lived in the country. One night, they heard footsteps outside the window. Three men were planning to rob the house!

2   Tenal shouted, "I heard there are robbers nearby."

3   His wife shouted back, "We must hide our gold. Let's put it in the well. No one will find it there."

4   Tenal and his wife carried many loads and dropped them into the well. Later, the robbers went to the well. They hauled up buckets of water and poured it in the garden. Finally, the well was empty. They looked down, but all they saw were stones!

5   Then the robbers saw Tenal and his wife standing nearby. The men were afraid. One said, "Don't put us in jail! We are sorry."

6   Tenal said, "You have helped me by watering my garden. I will let you go if you never steal again."

7   And the robbers never robbed anyone again.

✓ **Comprehension Questions**

1.   **Where does this story take place? Underline the sentence that tells.**

2.   **Where is Tenal at the beginning of the story?**

3.   **Where do Tenal and his wife catch the robbers?**   ___/3

Name _____ Date _____

Directions: Read the passage and answer the questions.
Write your answers on separate paper or on the back of this page.

Ravi's Bear

1   Ravi's mom bought her a stuffed bear at the
store. Then Ravi took a bus home, but she left the
bear on the bus. When she returned home, the toy
was missing!

2   The bus driver saw the bear. He stuffed it into his
backpack, but it fell out onto the sidewalk.

3   A boy on a bicycle saw the bear and stopped.
He put the bear in his basket and rode to the park.
While he was playing, a dog pulled the bear out of
the basket and ran.

4   A man was delivering groceries. He stopped the
dog and took the bear from it. Holding the bear
under his arm, he delivered groceries to a house.

5   Ravi answered the door. "Mama!" she cried. "The
grocery man is here, and he has my bear!" The
man smiled happily and handed the bear to Ravi.

✓ **Comprehension Questions**

1.   Where did Ravi get a stuffed bear? Underline the sentence that tells.

2.   Where did the bus driver put the bear?

3.   How did the dog get the bear?

4.   Circle the sentence that tells how Ravi got her
bear back in the end.

_____/4

Name _____ Date _____

Directions: Read the passage and answer the questions.
Write your answers on separate paper or on the back of this page.

The Day Snake Flew

1   Snake could climb trees and swim in the river.
     But he was not happy because he wanted to fly.

2   One day, Snake saw Eagle flying high in the air.
     He should have hidden, but he could not take his
     eyes off the bird. Eagle spotted Snake and grabbed
     him in her claws. Then she soared up into the air.

3   "Good thing I saw you!" Eagle said. "I'm hungry!"

4   Snake was scared and tried to get free. He swung
     his body this way and that. He screamed for help.

5   Eagle flew toward her nest. When she got near,
     her babies became afraid. Snake was thrashing
     back and forth and yelling. One eaglet tried to fly
     out of the nest. Of course, she was too young to fly.

6   So Eagle had to drop Snake to rescue her baby.
     She caught her eaglet and returned to the nest.

7   Snake landed on the ground and was very glad
     to be there. He never wanted to fly after that.

✓ **Comprehension Questions**

1.   **Why was Snake unhappy at the beginning? Underline the sentence that tells.**

2.   **How did Eagle catch Snake?**

3.   **What did Eagle plan to do with Snake?**

4.   **How did Snake get away from Eagle?**   ___/4

Name _____ Date _____

Directions: Read the passage and answer the questions.
Write your answers on separate paper or on the back of this page.

City Mouse and Country Mouse

1   One day, City Mouse went to visit his friend in the country. Country Mouse was poor, and he led a quiet life. But he brought out the best foods he had. He served a few bits of cheese, and a crust of bread.

2   City Mouse was used to very fine foods indeed. He could hardly eat what his friend offered.

3   "My friend," said City Mouse. "I don't know how you can live in this place. You should come to the city. We will eat like kings!"

4   Country Mouse agreed. So the two friends left that night and traveled to the city. They arrived at City Mouse's fine home just in time to enjoy the leftovers from a wonderful dinner.

5   Just as they were beginning to eat, the door of the room opened. In came a little boy and a huge dog. The dog raced after the two mice, who barely escaped back into their hole.

6   "Oh, my," said Country Mouse. "I don't know how you can live in this place. It's much too exciting for me. I would rather live in my quiet home and have a crust of bread than live here with such frightening things."

32

Jake and Pedro

1   Jake and Pedro were good friends. But Pedro had moved to the city two years ago and had not been back since. Today, Pedro was coming to visit.

2   When Jake opened the door of his family's small home, Pedro looked surprised. Pedro looked at the sandwiches Jake had made for lunch and made a funny face. Jake invited him to sit down and eat, but Pedro barely touched his food.

3   "My friend, you should come to the city with me," said Pedro. "You will love our big apartment, and we will eat some excellent food."

4   Jake had never been to the city, so he agreed. They rode a train to the city. As they left the train station, a taxi almost ran Jake over. Drivers blasted their horns at Jake. A man on a bike yelled at him.

5   "Oh, my," said Jake. "I don't know how you can live here. The city is much too noisy and dangerous for me."

 Comprehension Questions

1. **How are the main characters in the first story different from the characters in the second story?**

2. **How are the settings in these stories different?**

3. **What happens at the beginning of each story?**

4. **How are the characters in the first story like the characters in the second story?**

5. **What happens at the end of each story?**

_____/5

Name _____ Date _____

Directions: Read the passages and answer the questions.
Write your answers on separate paper or on the back of this page.

Lemonade Man

1   Kenji could not remember a summer as hot as this one. Every day seemed hotter than the day before. The people who walked by looked hot and tired.

2   Kenji had nothing to do and no money to spend. But then he got an idea. He could sell lemonade! On Monday morning, he got up early and made a huge jug of lemonade. He set up a little lemonade stand in front of his house and made a sign: "Lemonade $1.00."

3   Just before the morning rush began, Kenji went back into the house to get the cold lemonade. He picked up the jug and held it carefully in both hands as he walked outside to his stand. Along the way, he began thinking. "I could make a lot of money selling lemonade," he thought. "At $1.00 per glass, I could make at least $100 a day. Then I could buy those games I want, and I could go to the movies."

4   At that moment, Kenji's imagination got in his way, and he tripped on the sidewalk. The jug crashed to the ground, and all the lemonade poured out. And that was the end of Kenji's daydream.

The Milkmaid

1   Saturday was market day. Camille got up early and ate a quick breakfast. Then she went to do her chores on the farm. Finally, she filled a large pail with milk from the cows. She balanced the pail on her head and began walking to market.

2   As she walked, Camille started thinking. "I will sell this milk," she thought, "and buy some eggs. The eggs will hatch into chickens. Then I can sell the chickens at the market. I will make so much money that I can buy some new clothes. Then I will travel by coach to the city and find my fortune."

3   As Camille imagined leaving the farm at last, she gave her head a little toss. The pail of milk tipped over, and all the milk spilled on the ground. And that was the end of her imaginary plans.

 Comprehension Questions

1.   How are the main characters different in these two stories?

2.   How are the settings in these stories different?

3.   What happens at the beginning of each story?

4.   How are the characters in these stories alike?

_____/5

5.   What happens at the end of each story?

Name _____ Date _____

Directions: Read the passage and answer the questions.
Write your answers on separate paper or on the back of this page.

The Youngest Climber

1   Jordan Romero reached the top of the world on May 22, 2010. He was thirteen years old when he climbed the world's tallest mountain. That is Mount Everest in Nepal. It is more than 29,000 feet high, or about 5 ½ miles. Climbing to the top is very hard to do. Few people have done it.

2   When Jordan was ten, he saw a painting at his school. It showed the seven highest mountains in the world. He wanted to climb them. He told his father about his dream. His father agreed, and they began to train.

3   Over five years, Jordan climbed all seven mountains. He climbed Mount Everest with his father and stepmother. He was the youngest person ever to climb Mount Everest. He was also the youngest to complete all seven.

 Comprehension Questions

1.   **Who climbed Mount Everest with Jordan Romero?**
     Underline the sentence that tells.

2.   **When did Jordan climb Mount Everest?**
     Circle the sentence that tells.

3.   **Where is Mount Everest?**

4.   **What other mountains did Jordan climb?**

____/4

Name _____ Date _____

Directions: Read the passage and answer the questions.
Write your answers on separate paper or on the back of this page.

A Big Dinosaur

1   The titanosaur was the largest animal to walk on Earth. It weighed about 70 tons—more than 14 elephants! It was longer than two trucks, end to end.

2   When scientists found the bones of this dinosaur in Argentina in 2014, they got excited. They wanted to display them. But how do you show bones that stretch 122 feet long? The American Museum of Natural History in New York City decided to try.

3   Real bones are too heavy to hang together. The scientists made new bones in the same shapes and sizes. Then they put them together in a skeleton.

4   Next, they looked for a good place to put it. They put the body in one large room. Its head and neck reached into another one!

5   In January 2016, the dinosaur was ready. Many people went to the museum to see it.

✓ **Comprehension Questions**

1.   **How big was titanosaur? Underline <u>two</u> sentences that tell.**

2.   **Where was the titanosaur displayed?**

3.   **When did the show open?**

4.   **How did scientists make the titanosaur skeleton?**

____/5

Name _____ Date _____

Directions: Read the passage and answer the questions.
Write your answers on separate paper or on the back of this page.

Inside a Cactus

1   A cactus is an amazing plant. It lives in the very dry desert. The desert gets very little rain, but the cactus has all the water it needs.

2   A cactus has many roots near the top of the soil. When it does rain, the roots suck up the water as soon as it falls. Some kinds of cactus have long thick roots. When it doesn't rain, these roots search for water deep in the ground. Then the water runs up into the plant.

3   The cactus has a very tough skin. A waxy covering keeps the water inside. It has prickly thorns to keep animals away.

4   A huge cactus can hold as much water as a bathtub. But it is not pure water, like you get from the faucet. It is a thick liquid. It would be hard to pour into a glass!

 Comprehension Questions

1. **How does a cactus get water? Underline <u>two</u> sentences that tell.**
2. **What keeps animals away from a cactus?**
   Circle the sentence that tells.
3. **What is the outside of a cactus like?**
4. **What is the "water" like inside a cactus?**

_____/5

Name _____ Date _____

Directions: Read the passage and answer the questions.
Write your answers on separate paper or on the back of this page.

Flying High

1   Long before airplanes, people invented hot-air balloons. The science was simple. Air inside the balloon was heated. Hot air becomes lighter, so the balloon rose upward. A basket tied to the balloon carried passengers.

2   The first hot-air balloon flew in 1783. But there were no people in it. Instead, the passengers were a duck, a sheep, and a rooster. The flight was successful.

3   If a duck could fly safely, why couldn't a person? Jean-François de Rozier of France wanted to find out. So he got into a balloon. He tied a rope to the ground in case the balloon flew away. He heated air inside the balloon. Then he floated up high in the sky. He stayed up for 4 minutes. He was the first man ever to fly above the ground!

✔   **Comprehension Questions**

1.   **What passengers flew in the first successful balloon flight? Underline the sentence that tells.**

2.   **When did the first balloon flight happen? Circle the sentence that tells.**

3.   **How long did de Rozier stay in the air on his first flight?**

4.   **What did de Rozier do to his balloon for safety?**

_____/4

Name _____ Date _____

Directions: Read the passage and answer the questions.
Write your answers on separate paper or on the back of this page.

Amy's Tree House

1   Amy Carter was nine years old when her family moved into the White House in Washington, D.C. Her father, Jimmy Carter, had just become the President.

2   President Carter wanted Amy to be happy and have a normal childhood. She rode a bike and went to school. She got a dog called Grits. So when Amy asked for a tree house, her dad said okay.

3   He and Amy started working on the tree house. First, they found a good spot for it. Then President Carter asked one of the White House carpenters to build the house. But he did not want the house sitting on branches. He wanted posts to hold it up. That way, the tree would not be hurt.

4   Amy often played in her tree house. She invited her friends to play with her. Sometimes she invited friends for sleepovers—just like any other child.

 Comprehension Questions

1.   **What is the main topic of paragraph 2?
Underline the sentence that tells.**

2.   **What is paragraph 3 mostly about?**

3.   **What is the topic of the last paragraph?
Circle the sentence that tells.**

____/3

Name _____ Date _____

Directions: Read the passage and answer the questions.
Write your answers on separate paper or on the back of this page.

Moon Walk

1   What is it like to walk on the moon?

2   The moon is very different from Earth. There is no air to breathe. You have to carry a tank of air. It is either horribly hot or very cold on the moon. You have to wear a space suit to protect you from the heat and cold.

3   Gravity is not very strong on the moon. You can jump six times higher than you can jump on Earth. You have to be careful walking, though. If you walk on the moon like you do on Earth, you will fly up in the air and then fall over. So you have to take small hopping steps.

4   People walked on the moon many years ago. The first time was in 1969. But the moon has not changed since then.

✓ **Comprehension Questions**

1. **What is the main topic of paragraph 2?**
   Underline the sentence that tells.

2. **What is paragraph 3 mostly about?**

3. **What is the main topic of the last paragraph?**
   Circle the sentence that tells.

_____/3

Name _____ Date _____

Directions: Read the passage and answer the questions.
Write your answers on separate paper or on the back of this page.

Sharks

1   Sharks have been around for over 400 million years. There are about 375 kinds of sharks. Sharks are important for our oceans. They help clean the oceans. They eat older and slower fish and other sea animals.

2   People kill more than 200 million sharks every year. Some people kill sharks for food or to make money. Others think sharks are dangerous. They want to get rid of sharks.

3   If we don't stop killing sharks, they will disappear. Then our oceans will not be as healthy. One example of how this works is a fish called a cow nose ray. Some sharks like to eat rays. Rays like to eat scallops. But scallops keep the water clean. If the sharks die, then there will be too many rays. The rays will eat too many scallops. Then the water will become dirty.

✔ **Comprehension Questions**

1. **What is the main topic of paragraph 1? Underline the sentence.**
2. **Circle the main topic of paragraph 2.**
3. **Write a new title for this passage that gives the main topic.**

_____/3

Name _____ Date _____

Directions: Read the passage and answer the questions.
Write your answers on separate paper or on the back of this page.

Unusual Birds

1   When we think of birds, we think of creatures that fly. But there are some birds that don't fly. They have wings, but they stay on the ground.

2   The ostrich is one bird that cannot fly. It is the world's biggest and tallest bird. It can't fly, but it can run very fast. The ostrich holds its wings out when it runs. This helps the bird keep its balance.

3   Penguins are also birds that can't fly. They are great swimmers, though. They live in the coldest places on Earth. The penguin uses its wings to help it walk and swim.

4   The kiwi is a bird about the size of a chicken. The kiwi's wings are too small to fly, but it has strong feet and sharp claws. Like the ostrich, it can run very fast.

✔ **Comprehension Questions**

1.   **What is the main topic of paragraph 2? Underline the sentence.**

2.   **Circle the main topic of paragraph 3.**

3.   **Write a new title for this passage that gives the main topic.**

____/3

Name _____ Date _____

Directions: Read the passage and answer the questions.
Write your answers on separate paper or on the back of this page.

No King for America

1   George Washington was our first president. In those days, kings and queens ruled most countries. So why did America want a president and not a king or queen?

2   For a long time, America was ruled by England. Americans had few rights. They had to pay taxes to England. They had to follow English laws. King George III ruled England, and Americans thought he was unfair. Besides, no one voted for King George. He was born into a certain family and became king for life.

3   In 1775, America started a war against England. After the war, America became a nation on its own. The country needed a leader.

4   Some people wanted George Washington to become king. But most Americans wanted to vote. They chose Washington to be president.

 Comprehension Questions

1.   **Why didn't Americans like King George III?**
     Underline <u>two</u> sentences that explain.

2.   **How did America become free?**

3.   **Why did the United States choose a president instead of a king?**
     Circle the sentence that explains.

         ____/4

          Grade 2 • Benchmark Advance • **Reading** Quick Checks • © Benchmark Education Company, LLC

Name _____ Date _____

Directions: Read the passage and answer the questions.
Write your answers on separate paper or on the back of this page.

Here Comes the Mail!

1   Today, we get mail delivered almost every day. But mail has not always traveled fast. The first mail was delivered by people on foot or by horseback. It could take a month or more to get from one place to another.

2   The Pony Express began delivering mail in 1861. Riders on horseback traveled 75 to 100 miles a day. Mail arrived within ten days. But the Pony Express cost a lot. It ran for only about a year. Then trains took its place.

3   Trains were good for moving mail. The postal service sorted the mail at stops along the way. Mail could travel across the country in a few days.

4   In the 1900s, airplanes were invented. Airplanes are fast, and they can carry tons of mail. Now, packages and letters can cross the country in less than a day.

✔ **Comprehension Questions**

1.   **Why was mail so slow in the beginning? Underline the sentence that explains.**

2.   **Why did the Pony Express end? Circle two reasons.**

3.   **How fast could mail travel across the country by train?**

4.   **How are airplanes better than trains for carrying mail?**

____/5

Name _____ Date _____

Directions: Read the passage and answer the questions.
Write your answers on separate paper or on the back of this page.

Flying High

1   Long before airplanes, people invented hot-air balloons. The science was simple. Air inside the balloon was heated. Hot air becomes lighter, so the balloon rose upward. A basket tied to the balloon carried passengers.

2   The first hot-air balloon flew in 1783. But there were no people in it. Instead, the passengers were a duck, a sheep, and a rooster. The flight was successful.

3   If a duck could fly safely, why couldn't a person? Jean-François de Rozier of France wanted to find out. So he got into a balloon. He tied a rope to the ground in case the balloon flew away. He heated air inside the balloon. Then he floated up high in the sky. He stayed up for 4 minutes. He was the first man ever to fly above the ground!

 Comprehension Questions

1.   To fly a balloon, what was done first? Underline the sentence that tells.

2.   Why does a balloon go up? Circle the sentence that tells.

3.   What made de Rozier think people could fly in a balloon?

4.   Why did de Rozier tie a rope to his balloon?

_____/4

Name _____ Date _____

Directions: Read the passage and answer the questions.
Write your answers on separate paper or on the back of this page.

How a Seed Becomes a Plant

1   A seed is a small thing. Yet that seed can become a big plant. How does this happen?

2   Let's look at a bean. It is hard. A thin seed coat protects it. But if it's put in warm soil and given water, it changes. First, the seed coat gets soft. Then roots grow out and downward. Next, a small stem and two leaves come out of the seed. They grow up toward the sun. The roots are looking for water, and the leaves are looking for light.

3   All this time, the plant uses food from inside the seed. The food makes the leaves and roots grow.

4   Soon, the roots draw water from the soil. They also get materials that make food. With more sunshine and water, the plant grows more leaves. Then it makes more food inside the leaves. The plant grows and grows. In weeks, it will produce new beans.

✓ **Comprehension Questions**

1.   **What happens after the seed is put into warm soil and gets water?**
       Underline the sentence that tells.

2.   **What happens after the seed coat gets soft?**
       Circle two sentences that tell.

3.   **Why do roots grow down and the stem grows up?**   ____/5

4.   **What does a bean seed need to become a plant?**

Name _____ Date _____

Directions: Read the passage and answer the questions.
Write your answers on separate paper or on the back of this page.

How Soap Works

1   When you get dirty, you use soap to get clean. But how does soap work? Let's do an experiment. You will need a glass jar and some cooking oil.

2   Put a little cooking oil in the jar. Then mix in some water. Screw the lid on tight and shake the jar.

3   Watch the water and oil in the jar. After a minute or two, they will separate. The oil is in one layer, and the water is in another.

4   Now add some soap to the mixture and close the lid. Then shake it and let it sit for a few minutes.

5   Soon, the water becomes cloudy. The oil and soap have mixed together. Soap pulls the oil apart and makes it into tiny droplets. The oil is like dirt or grease on your body, or even on dishes. When the soap and oil mix, you can wash them both away.

✓ **Comprehension Questions**

1.   **What happens as a result of step 1? Underline the sentence that tells.**

2.   **What step comes after the water and oil separate in the jar?**

3.   **How can soap help you wash dirty dishes?**

_____/3

Name _____ Date _____

Directions: Read the passage and answer the questions.
Write your answers on separate paper or on the back of this page.

Reusing Plastic

1   When you recycle a plastic bottle, what happens to it? There are different kinds of plastic. So, first, the plastic must be sorted. Then sharp machines grind it up into tiny chips.

2   Plastic containers often are dirty. They might have glue, paper, or food on them. So the next step is to wash the plastic. Then it is dried in a big machine. After it dries, it is melted. Then the plastic is formed into tiny bits called pellets.

3   A company buys the pellets. They take truckloads of them to a factory. Then the plastic is used to make different things. Those things might include fleece jackets, carpet, floor mats, or tiles. They might be made into furniture, pipes, or pails. Reusing plastic makes good sense.

 Comprehension Questions

   1.   **Why is plastic sorted first? Underline the sentence that tells.**

   2.   **What happens just after the plastic is sorted? Circle the sentence that explains.**

   3.   **Why must plastic be washed?**

   4.   **Name four things made from recycled plastic.**

_____/4

Name _____ Date _____

Directions: Read the passage and answer the questions.
Write your answers on separate paper or on the back of this page.

The Flytrap

1 The Venus flytrap is an interesting plant. Unlike most plants, the flytrap eats meat. No, it doesn't eat beef or chicken. It eats <u>insects</u>.

2 Bugs crawl on the Venus flytrap because it gives off a sweet <u>scent</u>. A bug smells the plant and comes looking for food. Then it touches a hair on the leaf. Nothing happens until the insect <u>contacts</u> another hair. But if the bug touches a second hair, the plant moves. The two leaves clamp down and trap the bug. Then the plant covers the insect with juices. These juices help the plant <u>digest</u>, or take in and eat, the bug.

3 But why does the plant wait for the bug to touch two hairs? Sometimes things fall on the plant that are not bugs. If a twig falls on the plant, it doesn't move. The plant "knows" it cannot eat a twig.

 Comprehension Questions

Write the meaning of each of the four underlined words.
Circle a word or phrase in the passage that helps you find the meaning.

1. insects

2. scent

3. contacts   _____/8

4. digest

Name _____ Date _____

Directions: Read the passage and answer the questions.
Write your answers on separate paper or on the back of this page.

How We Use Wood

1   Wood is important in our lives. At home, your bed is probably wooden. Most furniture is made of wood. And what about your house? <u>Examine</u> your doorframes. Look at your windows or the outside of your house. Most likely, they are made of wood.

2   At school, you write on paper. Paper is made from wood. And look at the writing <u>utensil</u> you use. That pencil is a tool made of wood.

3   If you go to a <u>concert</u>, most of the musical instruments are made of wood. They include violins, pianos, and guitars. If you go to a baseball game, the bats are wood.

4   Some people use wood for heating. Trees are cut up for <u>firewood</u>. People burn the pieces in wood stoves.

 Comprehension Questions

Write the meaning of each of the four underlined words. Circle a word or phrase in the passage that helps you find the meaning.

1.   **examine**

2.   **utensil**

3.   **concert**   ___/8

4.   **firewood**

Name _____ Date _____

Directions: Read the passage and answer the questions.
Write your answers on separate paper or on the back of this page.

Amy's Tree House

1   Amy Carter was nine years old when her family <u>moved into</u> the White House in Washington, D.C. Her father, Jimmy Carter, had just become the President.

2   President Carter wanted Amy to be happy and have a normal childhood. She rode a bike and went to school. She got a dog called Grits. So when Amy asked for a tree house, her dad <u>said okay</u>.

3   He and Amy started working on the tree house. First, they found a <u>good spot</u> for it. Then President Carter asked one of the White House carpenters to build the house. But he did not want the house <u>sitting on</u> branches. He wanted posts to hold it up. That way, the tree would not be hurt.

4   Amy often played in her tree house. She invited her friends to play with her. Sometimes she invited friends for sleepovers—just like any other child.

 Comprehension Questions

Write the meaning of each of the four underlined phrases.
Circle a word or phrase in the passage that helps you find the meaning.

1. **moved into**
2. **said okay**
3. **good spot**
4. **sitting on**

____/8

Name _____ Date _____

Directions: Read the passage and answer the questions.
Write your answers on separate paper or on the back of this page.

Here Comes the Mail!

1   Today, we get mail delivered almost every day. But mail has not always traveled fast. The first mail was delivered by people <u>on foot</u> or by horseback. It could take a month or more to get from one place to another.

2   The Pony Express began delivering mail in 1861. Riders on horseback traveled 75 to 100 miles a day. Mail arrived within ten days. But the Pony Express cost a lot. <u>It ran</u> for only about a year. Then trains <u>took its place</u>.

3   Trains were good for moving mail. The postal service sorted the mail at stops along the way. Mail could travel across the country in a few days.

4   In the 1900s, airplanes were invented. Airplanes are fast, and they can carry <u>tons of</u> mail. Now, packages and letters can across the country in less than a day.

 Comprehension Questions

Write the meaning of each of the four underlined phrases.
Circle a word or phrase in the passage that helps you find the meaning.

1.   on foot
2.   It ran
3.   took its place
4.   tons of

____/8

Name _____ Date _____

Directions: Read the passage and answer the questions.
Write your answers on separate paper or on the back of this page.

Eat Your Seeds!

1   Seeds make great snacks. They are good for you, too. Eating seeds gives you energy. They are good for your heart and your skin. They are also quick and easy to eat.

Choosing the Right Seeds

2   You can't eat every seed. You have to choose the right ones. Some of the best seeds to eat are sunflower seeds and pumpkin seeds. Other seeds include nuts like pecans and peanuts.

Why Seeds Are Good for You

3   New plants grow from seeds. When a new plant grows, it uses the energy stored inside the seed. Eating that seed can put the energy inside you!

Look for "Raw"

4   Seeds are best eaten raw. That means they are not cooked. Cooking seeds takes away a lot of the good things inside. Look for seeds without salt or sugar, too.

 Comprehension Questions

1.   **Why are seeds good for you? Underline <u>two</u> sentences that explain.**

2.   **Circle <u>four</u> kinds of seeds that are good to eat.**

3.   **Under which heading can you find out why seeds should be eaten raw?**

_____/4

Name _____ Date _____

Directions: Read the passage and answer the questions.
Write your answers on separate paper or on the back of this page.

How Is a Baseball Made?

1   A baseball has three parts. Deep inside the baseball is a "pill." This piece of cork is a soft, woody ball. Two layers of rubber cover the cork.

2   After the cork is covered in rubber, it is covered with glue. Then yarn is wound tightly around the pill.

3   Last, the ball needs a cover. Two pieces of cowhide are glued over the yarn. Thick red thread sews the cowhide together.

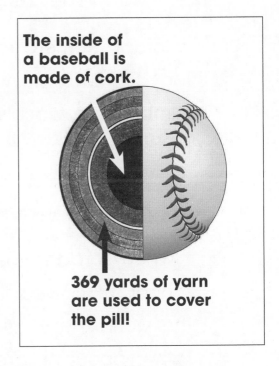

The inside of a baseball is made of cork.

369 yards of yarn are used to cover the pill!

The cover is sewed together with waxy thread.

 Comprehension Questions

1.   **What is inside a baseball? Circle the sentence that tells.**

2.   **What is wrapped around the pill inside the ball?**

3.   **How is the cover attached to the ball?**

4.   **How much yarn is used to make a baseball?**

____/4

Name _____ Date _____

Directions: Read the passage and answer the questions.
Write your answers on separate paper or on the back of this page.

The Youngest Climber

1   Jordan Romero reached the top of the world on May 22, 2010. He was thirteen years old when he climbed the world's tallest mountain. That is Mount Everest in Nepal. It is more than 29,000 feet high, or about 5 ½ miles. Climbing to the top is very hard to do. Few people have done it.

2   When Jordan was ten, he saw a painting at his school. It showed the seven highest mountains in the world. He wanted to climb them. He told his father about his dream. His father agreed, and they began to train.

3   Over five years, Jordan climbed all seven mountains. He climbed Mount Everest with his father and stepmother. He was the youngest person ever to climb Mount Everest. He was also the youngest to complete all seven.

✓ **Comprehension Questions**

1.   What is the author's purpose in this passage?

2.   Why did the author tell about the painting at school?

3.   Why did the author include paragraph 3?

____/3

Name _____ Date _____

Directions: Read the passage and answer the questions.
Write your answers on separate paper or on the back of this page.

Eat Your Seeds!

1   Seeds make great snacks. They are good for you, too. Eating seeds gives you energy. They are good for your heart and your skin. They are also quick and easy to eat.

2   You can't eat every seed. You have to choose the right ones. Some of the best seeds to eat are **sunflower** seeds and **pumpkin** seeds. Other seeds include nuts like **pecans** and **peanuts**.

3   New plants grow from seeds. When a new plant grows, it uses the energy stored inside the seed. Eating that seed can put the energy inside you!

4   Seeds are best eaten raw. That means they are not cooked. Cooking seeds takes away a lot of the good things inside. Look for seeds without salt or sugar, too.

Comprehension Questions

1.   **What is the author's purpose in this passage?**

2.   **Why did the author present some words in bold type?**

3.   **What is the purpose of paragraph 3?**

4.   **What is the purpose of paragraph 4?**

_____/4

Name _____ Date _____

Directions: Read the passage and answer the questions.
Write your answers on separate paper or on the back of this page.

Why Boats Float

1   Why does a stone sink but a boat floats? Think of a boat floating in the water. Some of the boat sits below the water. Yet most of the boat stays above the water. With the right shape, a boat will float. It can even carry things.

2   When a boat floats, it pushes down into the water. Scientists say that it "displaces" the water. That means it takes the water's place. At the same time, the water pushes up on the boat. As long as the boat weighs less than the water, it stays up. If the boat gets too heavy, it will sink.

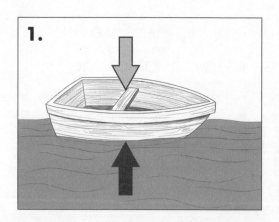 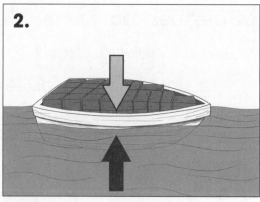

✓ **Comprehension Questions**

1. **What does picture 1 help you understand?**

2. **Which sentences in the passage are illustrated by the arrows in picture 1? Underline two sentences.**

3. **Circle the sentence that is illustrated by picture 2.**

____/4

Name _____ Date _____

Directions: Read the passage and answer the questions.
Write your answers on separate paper or on the back of this page.

Bluebirds

1   One of the most beautiful birds is the eastern bluebird. The males are blue on their wings, head, and tail. Their chests are brown and their bellies are white. The females have gray heads and brown bodies.

2   Bluebirds have round heads and large eyes. They are six to eight inches long. They weigh about as much as a slice of bread.

3   People enjoy watching bluebirds. They even put up bluebird houses to attract the birds. They place them in open places, such as meadows.

 Comprehension Questions

1.   **What does picture 1 show that bluebirds like to eat?**

2.   **What description of the birds in paragraph 2 is shown in picture 1?**

3.   **How does picture 2 help you understand the passage?**

____/3

Name _____ Date _____

Directions: Read the passage and answer the questions.
Write your answers on separate paper or on the back of this page.

Sharks

1   Sharks have been around for over 400 million years. There are about 375 kinds of sharks. Sharks are important for our oceans. They help clean the oceans. They eat older and slower fish and other sea animals.

2   People kill more than 200 million sharks every year. Some people kill sharks for food or to make money. Others think sharks are dangerous. They want to get rid of sharks.

3   If we don't stop killing sharks, they will disappear. Then our oceans will not be as healthy. One example of how this works is a fish called a cow nose ray. Some sharks like to eat rays. Rays like to eat scallops. But scallops keep the water clean. If the sharks die, then there will be too many rays. The rays will eat too many scallops. Then the water will become dirty.

 Comprehension Questions

1.   The passage says sharks are important for our oceans. Underline <u>two</u> sentences that give reasons.

2.   Circle <u>two</u> sentences that give reasons why people kill sharks.

3.   What reason does the author give to explain why we need sharks to eat cow nose rays?

_____/5

60

Name _____ Date _____

Directions: Read the passage and answer the questions.
Write your answers on separate paper or on the back of this page.

No King for America

1   George Washington was our first president. In those days, kings and queens ruled most countries. So why did America want a president and not a king or queen?

2   For a long time, America was ruled by England. Americans had few rights. They had to pay taxes to England. They had to follow English laws. King George III ruled England, and Americans thought he was unfair. Besides, no one voted for King George. He was born into a certain family and became king for life.

3   In 1775, America started a war against England. After the war, America became a nation on its own. The country needed a leader.

4   Some people wanted George Washington to become king. But most Americans wanted to vote. They chose Washington to be president.

✔ **Comprehension Questions**

1.   **For a long time, Americans were unhappy with England. Underline three reasons the author gives to explain why Americans were unhappy.**

2.   **Circle the sentence that tells why Americans made Washington president instead of king.**

____/4

Name _____ Date _____

Directions: Read the passages and answer the questions.
Write your answers on separate paper or on the back of this page.

Passage 1:
A Big Dinosaur

1   The titanosaur was the largest animal to walk on Earth. It weighed about 70 tons—more than 14 elephants! It was longer than two trucks, end to end.

2   When scientists found the bones of this dinosaur in Argentina in 2014, they got excited. They wanted to display them. But how do you show bones that stretch 122 feet long? The American Museum of Natural History in New York City decided to try.

3   Real bones are too heavy to hang together. The scientists made new bones in the same shapes and sizes. Then they put them together in a skeleton.

4   Next, they looked for a good place to put it. They put the body in one large room. Its head and neck reached into another one!

5   In January 2016, the dinosaur was ready. Many people went to the museum to see it.

Passage 2:
A Dinosaur Named Sue

1   On May 17, 2000, more than 10,000 people visited the Field Museum in Chicago. They wanted to see a new dinosaur skeleton named "Sue."

2   Sue was a T. rex. She lived 65 million years ago. She was 42 feet long and stood about 13 feet tall at the hip. She weighed about six tons. Her teeth were a foot long! The T. rex was fierce and very scary. It ran fast. It had an excellent sense of smell. Few animals could escape it.

3   Sue's bones were found in 1990. A woman named Sue Hendrickson found them in South Dakota. The T. rex was named after her. It is one of the most complete dinosaur skeletons ever found. Scientists have learned a lot from it.

 Comprehension Questions

1. **What is the main topic of Passage 1?**
2. **What is the main topic of Passage 2?**
3. **Describe <u>two</u> ways these passages are alike.**
4. **Name <u>two</u> pieces of information the author gives in Passage 2 that are not given in Passage 1.**

____/6

Name _____ Date _____

Directions: Read the passages and answer the questions.
Write your answers on separate paper or on the back of this page.

Passage 1:
Amy's Tree House

1   Amy Carter was nine years old when her family
moved into the White House in Washington, D.C.
Her father, Jimmy Carter, had just become
the President.

2   President Carter wanted Amy to be happy
and have a normal childhood. She rode a bike
and went to school. She got a dog called Grits.
So when Amy asked for a tree house, her dad
said okay.

3   He and Amy started working on the tree house.
First, they found a good spot for it. Then President
Carter asked one of the White House carpenters
to build the house. But he did not want the house
sitting on branches. He wanted posts to hold it
up. That way, the tree would not be hurt.

4   Amy often played in her tree house. She invited
her friends to play with her. Sometimes she invited
friends for sleepovers—just like any other child.

Passage 2:
Growing Up in the White House

1   Sasha Obama was seven years old when she moved into the White House. Her father had just been elected President, and her life was about to change.

2   Michelle and Barack Obama wanted Sasha to have a normal childhood. But people always want to know what she is doing. Newspapers are always looking for stories about her. So the Obamas kept Sasha away from cameras. They were careful what they tell the press about her.

3   Still, Sasha had a pretty normal childhood in the White House. She thought of it as home and lived there for eight years. In 2008, she and her sister got a dog named Bo. Later, they got a second dog named Sunny. Sasha also had sleepovers. She played basketball, and her father helped coach the team.

✔ **Comprehension Questions**

1. **What is the main topic of Passage 1?**
2. **What is the main topic of Passage 2?**
3. **Name <u>two</u> ways these passages are alike.**
4. **Name one thing that both Amy and Sasha did in the White House.**
5. **Name one thing Sasha did in the White House that Amy did not.**

___/6

Grade 2
Literature Answer Key

Ask Questions A (page 2)

1. "She hopped through the field and the woods looking here and there."
2. bees
3. a bear
4. "Rabbit felt a little sad because no one wanted her company."

Ask Questions B (page 3)

1. in Taki's home
2. "His room was piled with clothes and toys, so he put everything away."
3. He went to his brother's room.
4. "Then he looked for his dad in the kitchen."

Answer Questions A (page 4)

1. "Turtle lived in a pond with Frog."
2. "Turtle wanted to be friends, but Frog was not interested."
3. Frog is making fun of Turtle; Turtle is on his back and cannot move.
4. Turtle does not want to be friends with Frog.

Answer Questions B (page 5)

1. in Mouse's home
2. "One night as he went to bed, he wished his tail would grow."
3. He has a dream.
4. "Suddenly, Mouse's mother was shaking him."

Recount the Story A (page 6)

1. Ravi's mom buys her a stuffed bear.
2. The boy picks it up from the sidewalk.
3. He takes it from the dog.
4. When the man delivers groceries to Ravi's house, Ravi sees her bear.

Recount the Story B (page 7)

(4 points for an excellent recounting of the story that includes more than three events; 3 points for a proficient recounting that includes three events; 2 points for an adequate recounting with two important events; 1 point for an incomplete recounting with one important event.)

Sample recounting: Sammy is collecting acorns. Sally sees him and offers to help. After they finish collecting Sammy's acorns, Sammy finds out Sally doesn't have any acorns. He says that together they can collect her acorns in no time.

Identify the Message A (page 8)

1. "Crow wanted some peanuts."
2. They get angry and peck at him; they drive Crow away.
3. They are mean to him; they fly away and leave him alone.
4. "Crow decided, 'It's best just to be yourself.'"

Identify the Message B (page 9)

1. "The salt melted, and the donkey's load got much lighter."
2. He lay in the water on purpose.
3. His load got heavier because the man put sponges in his bag.
3. It is wrong to try to fool people over and over.

Describe How Characters Respond A (page 10)

1. (2 points) "He swung his body this way and that." and "He screamed for help."
2. She got scared and tried to fly out of the nest.
3. She dropped Snake to rescue her baby.
4. Snake felt glad, or relieved, or lucky.

Describe How Characters Respond B (page 11)

1. "So he took it to Ana's Bike Shop."
2. He went back to Ana's Bike Shop.
3. His brakes stopped working.
4. Ana offered Dan a job.

Identify Alliteration A (page 12)

(3 points; 1 point per verse for at least one set of words that use alliteration)

1. Waiting, watching
2. dives, dinner, Delightful / But, bunnies, bird
3. Hippity, hippity, / Hippity, hop

Identify Alliteration B (page 13)

(3 points; 1 point per verse for at least one set of words that use alliteration)

1. Polly, Pig, pen / left, little, lunch
2. beans, beets
3. Yippee, yelled / chunks, cheese

Identify Rhythm A (page 14)

1. (Stressed syllables are in bold.)

   A **poor** thing the **mouse** was, and **yet**,

   When the **Lion** got **caught** in a **net**,

   All his **strength** was no **use**,

   'Twas the **little** poor **mouse**

   Who **chewed** his way **out** of the **net**.

2. The last word in each line is emphasized.
   The same words/syllables are emphasized in each poem
   (because they are both limericks).
3. The first, second, and last lines rhyme.
   The third and fourth lines rhyme
   (although "use" and "mouse" in the first poem is marginal.)

Identify Rhythm B (page 15)
1. (Stressed syllables are in bold.)
   I will **be** the **glad**dest **thing**
       Un**der** the **sun**!
   I will **touch** a **hun**dred **flowers**
       And **not** pick **one**.
2. The first and third lines are long, and the second
   and fourth lines are short.
3. second and fourth in each verse

Determine Meaning Using Alliteration, Rhythm, Repetition A (page 16)
1. The butterfly does not sing.
2. "First it is a little grub,
   And then it is a nice yellow cocoon,
   And then the butterfly
   Eats its way out soon."
3. They do not sting and do not have a hive.
4. We should try to be good like butterflies.

Determine Meaning Using Alliteration, Rhythm, Repetition B (page 17)
1. Sample answer: "Yet there isn't a train goes by all day" and
   "Yet there isn't a train I wouldn't take,"
2. "But I see its cinders red on the sky,"
3. She likes her friends; she'll never know any better friends
   (although she would leave them in a second if a train comes by).
4. She loves trains. In the last two lines, she says she would take
   one anywhere.

Describe Beginnings of Stories A (page 18)
1. "Tanya wanted to play soccer with her brother Ray and his
   friends."
2. Tanya doesn't know how to play soccer.
3. Tanya plays soccer by herself.

Describe Beginnings of Stories B (page 19)
1. "When she walked by, they jumped out and surprised her."
2. She is scared.
3. She flies up into a tree.

Describe Endings of Stories A (page 20)
1. "Misha wanted to ride her new bike, but she was afraid."
2. He holds on to her bike as she rides.
3. Her father lets go, and Misha is riding on her own.

Describe Endings of Stories B (page 21)
1. "Three men were planning to rob the house!"
2. They pretend to put their gold in the well.
3. Tenal lets the robbers go. They agree to stop robbing people.

Describe Story Structure A (page 22)
1. "So it jumped on a deer to get warm."
2. (2 points) Flea jumps on the cow, and then she jumps on the dog.
3. The man puts the flea outside.

Describe Story Structure B (page 23)
1. "Monkey was very hungry, but he couldn't find any food."
2. Monkey needed to get across the river.
3. (2 points) Monkey steps on a crocodile, and then the crocodile calls all the other crocodiles.
4. Monkey crosses the river by walking on the crocodiles and eats some plums.

Identify Points of View A (page 24)
1. Rabbit feels curious.
2. The bees are angry.
3. The bear feels grumpy or upset.
4. Rabbit's mother is happy to see her.

Identify Points of View B (page 25)
1. Turtle wants to be friends with Frog.
2. Frog doesn't like it and gets upset.
3. Frog dares Turtle to swim on his back.
4. Turtle doesn't like Frog and does not want him as a friend.

Use Details to Understand Characters A (page 26)
1. "Tomorrow was Mom's birthday, and he wanted to buy her a birthday present."
2. (2 points) Taki cleans his room, and he washes the dishes in the kitchen.
3. "'This is the BEST birthday present ever!'"

Grade 2 • Benchmark Advance • **Reading** Quick Checks • © Benchmark Education Company, LLC

Use Details to Understand Characters B (page 27)

1. Dan listens to Ana and learns how to fix his bike.
2. (2 points) Ana shows Dan how to fix his bike and gives him tools.
3. "'You know a lot about bikes, and I need a helper!'"

Use Details to Understand Setting A (page 28)

1. "One day Crow saw a flock of pigeons in the town square."
2. He goes to the ground in the square.
3. "He spotted his flock in a tree and flew over to it."

Use Details to Understand Setting B (page 29)

1. "Tenal and his wife lived in the country."
2. Tenal is at home.
3. They catch the robbers outside by the well.

Use Details to Understand Plot A (page 30)

1. "Ravi's mom bought her a stuffed bear at the store."
2. The bus driver put the bear in his backpack.
3. The dog pulled the bear out of the boy's basket.
4. "The man smiled happily and handed the bear to Ravi."

Use Details to Understand Plot B (page 31)

1. "But he was not happy because he wanted to fly."
2. Eagle grabbed Snake with her claws while Snake was watching Eagle fly.
3. Eagle was going to eat Snake or feed Snake to her babies.
4. Snake squirmed and yelled. Eagle dropped him to save her baby.

Compare and Contrast Two Versions of a Story A (page 32)

1. The characters in the first story are mice, and the characters in the second story are humans.
2. The first story takes place in mouse homes; the second takes place in a person's home and on a busy city street.
3. The city character visits the country character.
4. One character lives in the country and enjoys a quiet life; the other lives in the city and enjoys a noisy, busy life.
5. The country character decides the city is too dangerous for him.

Compare and Contrast Two Versions of a Story B (page 34)

1. One is a boy, and the other is a girl.
2. One is set at a home in a city, and the other is on a farm.
3. Both characters get up early with a plan to make money.
4. Both characters dream of making a lot of money and what they will spend their money on.
5. Both characters spill the liquid that is supposed to help them earn money.

Informational Text Answer Key

Ask Questions to Demonstrate Understanding of Key Details A (page 36)

1. "He climbed Mount Everest with his father and stepmother."
2. "Jordan Romero reached the top of the world on May 22, 2010."
3. Mount Everest is in Nepal.
4. Jordan climbed the six other highest mountains in the world.

Ask Questions to Demonstrate Understanding of Key Details B (page 37)

1. (2 points) "It weighed about 70 tons—more than 14 elephants!" and "It was longer than two trucks, end to end."
2. The titanosaur was displayed in New York at the American Museum of Natural History.
3. The show opened in January 2016.
4. They used models of the bones.

Answer Questions to Demonstrate Understanding of Key Details A (page 38)

1. (2 points) "When it does rain, the roots suck up the water as soon as it falls." and "When it doesn't rain, these roots search for water deep in the ground."
2. "It has prickly thorns to keep animals away."
3. The skin is very tough and waxy.
4. It is a thick liquid.

Answer Questions to Demonstrate Understanding of Key Details B (page 39)

1. "Instead, the passengers were a duck, a sheep, and a rooster."
2. "The first hot-air balloon flew in 1783."
3. De Rozier stayed up for 4 minutes.
4. He tied a rope to the ground.

Identify Main Topic of a Paragraph A (page 40)

1. "President Carter wanted Amy to be happy and have a normal childhood."
2. Paragraph 3 is mostly about how President Carter and Amy built a tree house.
3. "Amy often played in her tree house."

Identify Main Topic of a Paragraph B (page 41)

1. "The moon is very different from Earth."
2. Paragraph 3 is mostly about gravity on the moon.
3. "People walked on the moon many years ago."

Grade 2 • Benchmark Advance • **Reading** Quick Checks • © Benchmark Education Company, LLC

Identify Main Topic of a Multi-Paragraph Text A (page 42)
1. "Sharks are important for our oceans."
2. "People kill more than 200 million sharks every year."
3. Sample answers: "We Need Sharks" OR "Save Our Sharks"

Identify Main Topic of a Multi-Paragraph Text B (page 43)
1. "The ostrich is one bird that cannot fly."
2. "Penguins are also birds that can't fly."
3. Sample Answer: "Birds That Don't Fly"

Describe Connections in a Historical Text A (page 44)
1. (2 points) "King George III ruled England, and Americans thought he was unfair." and "Besides, no one voted for King George."
2. America won a war against England.
3. "But most Americans wanted to vote."

Describe Connections in a Historical Text B (page 45)
1. "The first mail was delivered by people on foot or by horseback."
2. (2 points) "But the Pony Express cost a lot." "Then trains took its place."
3. "Mail could travel across the country in a few days."
4. Airplanes are faster than trains.

Describe Connections in a Scientific Text A (page 46)
1. "Air inside the balloon was heated."
2. "Hot air becomes lighter, so the balloon rose upward."
3. Since animals were able to fly in a balloon, he thought that people could, too.
4. De Rozier tied a rope to his balloon so that he wouldn't fly away.

Describe Connections in a Scientific Text B (page 47)
1. "First, the seed coat gets soft."
2. (2 points) "Then roots grow out and downward." and "Next, a small stem and two leaves come out of the seed."
3. The roots are looking for water, and the leaves are looking for light.
4. A seed needs soil, water, and sunlight.

Describe Connections in a Technical Text A (page 48)
1. "After a minute or two, they will separate."
2. Add soap to the mixture, close the lid, and shake it.
3. Soap pulls the oil apart so it washes away.

Describe Connections in a Technical Text B (page 49)
1. "There are different kinds of plastic."
2. "Then sharp machines grind it up into tiny chips."
3. It must be washed to get rid of any glue, paper, or food.
4. fleece jackets, carpet, floor mats, tiles

Determine the Meaning of Words A (page 50)
1. (2 points) bugs / "Bugs crawl"
2. (2 points) smell / "smells the plant"
3. (2 points) touches / "touches a hair"
4. (2 points) break down the food; absorb / "take in and eat"

Determine the Meaning of Words B (page 51)
1. (2 points) look closely / "Look at"
2. (2 points) tool / "a tool"
3. (2 points) musical show / "musical instruments"
4. (2 points) wood that is cut up and burned / "Trees are cut up"; "burn the pieces"

Determine the Meaning of Phrases A (page 52)
1. (2 points) lived / "White House"
2. (2 points) approved; said yes / "So when Amy asked"
3. (2 points) good place or location / "found"
4. (2 points) resting on; supported by / "posts to hold it up"

Determine the Meaning of Phrases B (page 53)
1. (2 points) walking / "or by horseback"
2. (2 points) operated; worked; continued / "only about a year"
3. (2 points) replaced it / "Then trains"
4. (2 points) a lot of; large amounts / "can carry"

Use Text Features to Locate Information A (page 54)
1. (2 points) "When a new plant grows, it uses the energy stored inside the seed." and "Eating that seed can put the energy inside you!"
2. sunflower seeds, pumpkin seeds, pecans, peanuts
3. "Look for 'Raw'"

Use Text Features to Locate Information B (page 55)
1. "The inside of a baseball is made of cork." (label)
2. Yarn is wrapped around the pill inside the ball.
3. The cover is attached with glue, and then it is sewn with thread.
4. 369 yards of yarn are used to make a baseball. (label)

Identify Author's Purpose A (page 56)

1. The author's purpose is to give information about Jordan Romero.
2. The author told about to the painting to explain how Jordan got the idea to climb mountains.
3. Paragraph 3 describes what Jordan did.

Identify Author's Purpose B (page 57)

1. The author's purpose is to encourage the reader to eat seeds.
2. The bold words show which seeds are best for you.
3. The purpose is to explain why seeds are good for you, or give you energy.
4. The purpose is to explain why seeds should be eaten raw.

Explain How Images Contribute to a Text A (page 58)

1. It shows why a boat floats.
2. (2 points) "When a boat floats, it pushes down into the water." and "At the same time, the water pushes up on the boat."
3. "It can even carry things." OR "If the boat gets too heavy, it will sink."

Explain How Images Contribute to a Text B (page 59)

1. They like to eat berries.
2. "Bluebirds have round heads and large eyes."
3. It shows what bluebird houses look like.

Describe Reasons in Text That Support Author's Points A (page 60)

1. (2 points) "They help clean the oceans." and "They eat older and slower fish and other sea animals."
2. (2 points) "Some people kill sharks for food or to make money." and "Others think sharks are dangerous."
3. Without sharks to eat cow nose rays, too many scallops will be eaten and the water will get dirty.

Describe Reasons in Text That Support Author's Points B (page 61)

1. (3 points) "Americans had few rights."
   "They had to pay taxes to England."
   "They had to follow English laws."
2. "But most Americans wanted to vote."

Compare and Contrast Two Texts on a Topic A (page 62)
1. The main topic is the titanosaur.
2. The main topic is Sue, the T. rex.
3. (2 points) They describe dinosaurs and they tell about a skeleton in a museum.
4. (2 points) The second passage tells how long ago Sue lived, and it tells who found the bones.

Compare and Contrast Two Texts on a Topic B (page 64)
1. The main topic is Amy Carter and her tree house.
2. The main topic is Sasha Obama.
3. (2 points) They both describe girls who lived in the White House, and they both describe how their parents wanted them to have a normal childhood.
4. Sample answer: had sleepovers
5. Sasha played basketball.